MARLESE JOHNSON

BIPOLAR DISORDER

The Ultimate Guide on the Truth About Bipolar Disorder,
Discover All The Important Information About Bipolar
Disorder and What You Can Do To Manage It

Descrierea CIP a Bibliotecii Naţionale a României
MARLESE JOHNSON
  BIPOLAR DISORDER. The Ultimate Guide on the Truth
About Bipolar Disorder, Discover All The Important
Information About Bipolar Disorder and What You Can Do To
Manage It / Marlese Johnson. – Bucharest: Editura My Ebook, 2020
  ISBN

MARLESE JOHNSON

BIPOLAR DISORDER

**The Ultimate Guide on the Truth About Bipolar Disorder,
Discover All The Important Information About Bipolar
Disorder and What You Can Do To Manage It**

My Ebook Publishing House
Bucharest, 2020

TABLE OF CONTENTS

INTRODUCTION

Bipolar is a condition that wreaks havoc on those that it affects. If you suffer from Bipolar, chances are that your family suffers right with you. No matter if you are that family member trying to learn to cope or you are the person that has been diagnosised, there is hope out there.

Although there is no cure for Bipolar, just yet, there are many ways in which you can improve your chances of living a long and happy life. The good news is that the process doesn't have to be difficult either.

The ups and downs are what make the most problems for individuals. Being happy and go lucky one minute is wonderful but when it is followed by serious lows and depressed moods the next, there's even more to worry about.

In this e-book, you will find a number of different scenarios that will help you to ultimately learn to cope with bipolar and all of these ups and downs. Through an understanding of your condition as well as help in dealing with the beneficial tools we will teach you, you will be able to improve the quality of life that you and your loved ones share.

CHAPTER 1

UNDERSTANDING BIPOLAR

Most individuals that suffer from bipolar have one simple goal. That goal is to live a life that is as normal as can be. To get through today without having any emotional problems, to make it through the big meeting at work without having people wonder what is wrong with you and to simply be able to enjoy your daughter's graduation are all additional goals that you may have.

Before you can fully learn to cope with bipolar, you need to fully understand your condition. You need to know what things happen, as best that you can, so that you can then trigger your coping mechanisms to work for you.

There is no 100 percent sure way of stopping these things from happening to you. But, there are countless things you can learn to do to help you to improve your outlook.

To get to that point, we will start by giving you all of the information you need about your condition so that you can better understand what is happening to you. If you are a family member who just wants to help someone that has bipolar, then by all means, you too can learn all that you need to in order to deliver the help that you can give to them.

Bipolar: The Medical Side

Bipolar is a condition in which there are extremes in moods and life experiences. There is no doubt that bipolar is a health condition that is serious and disabling to those that have it. It is a mental illness and it does require necessary treatment.

You may have heard bipolar called Manic Depression or that a person suffering from it has a manic depressive condition. But, what scientists have come to learn is that manic style behavior is only one extreme of this condition. The other part of it is that of depression. Both of these conditions are vitally serious to your well being and even to your life span and must be treated.

While doctors do not have a cause for bipolar, they are working on finding one. Along with that, you can be sure that there are many scientists looking for a way to cure the condition.

Yet, until that happens, we need to examine what we do know about bipolar and what it does to the person that you are.

For most people bipolar starts when they are just in their teens. Some believe that it is triggered by puberty. Others will not develop this condition until they are in their early adult years. Bipolar can last your life time, too.

For most individuals, bipolar is a condition that doesn't happen all of the time. You don't go in and out of moods ore other experiences within seconds and you don't do this all of the time either. For example, some people will have bouts that last for several weeks. Others will have them for a few months at a time. Although it is possible to have bipolar in which your symptoms flare all of the time, this is really the rare case.

If you don't get help for bipolar, your condition is likely to continue to worsen. There is no doubt that depression itself is a killer. Therefore, not getting help is simply not an option. But, the good news is that there are medications, treatments and therapies that can help to reduce the symptoms and help you to cope with your condition.

Do You Have Bipolar?

The first question that you need to ask is if you have this condition. Learning the signs and symptoms will help you to weigh the need to seek out medical attention. If any of your symptoms are severe or you are considering harming yourself, you must seek immediate medical attention as soon as possible.

Bipolar individuals will go through an alternating pattern of highs and lows that play on their emotions. The highs are called episodes of mania.

The lows are episodes of depression. The intensity of these highs and lows will vary from person to person and from one episode to the next. For some, the symptoms can be quite mild but for others they can be quite severe. In addition to this, you may also have very normal times too.

During the manic phase, there are a number of symptoms that can be observed.

- You may feel extremely happy and optimistic. You may feel euphoria. You may also have an inflated self esteem or ego, too.

- You may have very poor judgment, and you may know this by being told by others that you've made the wrong decision.

- Your speech can be very fast. Your mind is going crazy with thoughts. You may be agitated and feel the need to move your body and your mind. Physical activity may be increased, too.

- Many will be aggressive in their behavior, often more so than is "allowable."

- Some people find this to be a time of problems with sleeping, problems with concentrating one what you should be doing. You may be easily distracted, and have problems getting tasks accomplished.

- You can be reckless or you may take chances on things that you normally would not do.

Those that suffer from the mania side of bipolar will transition from it into the depressive side. The depressive side is that which people often associated with depression like symptoms. These symptoms can include the following, more than one, too.

The depressive bipolar symptoms include:

- Feeling very sad, very guilty or feeling that all is lost. Hopelessness is a common feeling here too. The trademark of a problem is that the symptom is unfounded and is persistent.

- You may be very tired, often not caring about getting your tasks accomplished. You may lose interest in the things that you do daily, normally. Even those things that you love to do may not be done.

- You may be very irritable, losing your temper for no real reason.

- You may not be able to sleep although you are tired. You may not be hungry and some will lose weight because of not eating properly here.

- Some have problems with pain, too. If you have pain that there is no real cause for, this can be a sign of depressive behavior.

- The most serious of all symptoms and signs of depressive behavior is that of thoughts of suicide. If you have these thoughts, your condition needs immediate attention.

If you think that you have any of these symptoms, then you need to work with your doctor to be diagnosised. It is necessary to get treatment and treatment really can help you!

What's The Cause?

The one thing that all bipolar patients want to know is why.

Why did this happen to me? Why do I go through this? Why can't my life be normal?

Unfortunately, there just is not an answer to that. Neither doctors nor scientists understand why or what causes bipolar to happen. But, they have some ideas of what could be behind the way you feel.

Most believe that it is a combination of factors that lead to this condition including environmental, genetics, and biological factors. Doctors believe that these conditions not only cause the onset of bipolar in people but also control when the episodes that you experience happen and how frequently they do.

Those that have bipolar have problems within the brain. There are chemical messengers in your brain that go between the nerve cells and the brain itself relaying information. These are called neurotransmitters.

In those that have bipolar, those messengers are somehow different and simply communicate in a different way to the brain triggering the symptoms that you face.

It is believed that those that suffer from bipolar have a genetic code that puts them in that position. While this genetic disposition doesn't per say actually trigger the condition to happen, those that have this coding actually have a better chance of developing it at some point in their lives.

This difference in the neurotransmitters is believed to have to do with an abnormal aspect of the genes. Your genes that control the neurotransmitters in your brain simply developed abnormally, leading to bipolar. But, remember, just because this is the case, it doesn't mean that you are going to suffer from bipolar. It just means that it is something that you could experience.

In addition to this genetic code, most doctors believe that it is necessary for you to have some environmental effects to happen in order to trigger the problem. This can include such things as drug abuse and very stressful events. Sometimes, a very traumatic event especially those that are psychological can trigger bipolar.

Are You At Risk?

You may be at risk for bipolar if you have a family history of bipolar or other depressive conditions. In fact, in up to 90 percent of those with bipolar there is evidence of depression in the family.

Again, if you have genes that are passed down from those in your family that have these abnormalities, then you are more likely to experience bipolar.

While the exact genes are not know just yet, there are many researchers working on finding the gene that makes you more or less likely to have bipolar disorder.

Should You Go To The Doctor?

If you are reading this far into this book, then you probably realize the importance of seeking medical attention for your condition. The problem is that most that have symptoms of bipolar don't realize that they do have a problem.

Some will realize that something is not right but most will not realize just how impaired they are. In addition, most don't realize just how troublesome going through these mood swings can be for other family members. You probably don't realize what you are putting your family and friends through.

Therefore, it often takes someone else, such as your spouse, friend or other relatives to help you to get to the doctor so that you can be diagnosed for your own safety and health. Those that are concerned about their loved ones should seek the help that they need. Professional help can be quite beneficial to those that are suffering.

If a person that is suffering from bipolar does not seek out and get the help that he or she needs, not only will stresses continue to build, but physical problems can also become evident. They can be hurt in one of their episodes.

Who Should I See?

If you realize the need to seek professional help, your first contact should be your family doctor. He or she can help you to determine that there are no other medical problems causing your condition. From here, though, the person to see is that of a psychiatrist.

Do not worry; the process of seeking help in dealing with any type of mental illness including depression and bipolar syndrome is quite simple to do.

Take a loved one with you that has noticed the symptoms that you are experiencing. The first thing that your doctor will ask is what type of symptoms you are having. He or she will ask you to describe both the depressive symptoms and the mania symptoms.

During your first meeting with the doctor, you'll talk about your daily life, the episodes you are experiencing and your overall health. The first thing that he or she will do is work on ruling out other medical problems and other mental health problems. Other conditions, such as mood disorders, attention deficit hyperactivity disorder, schizophrenia, and even a personality disorder, can have similar symptoms to bipolar conditions.

Your doctor may also ask you to undergo tests that will determine if there are any other things that causing your condition. He or she will want to find out if you have physical causes to your bipolar disorder (or the likely diagnosis of this.)

This can include talking about substance abuse. Your doctor will ask and need an honest opinion about this. If you drink alcohol, use illegal drugs such as marijuana and cocaine, then you need to tell your doctor about these things. Remember, your doctor can't talk about this with anyone else.

These types of drugs can alter the mood and in some people create larger fluctuations of moods.

Another possible reason for your mood swings can be due to health problems like thyroid disorders. Here, a blood test will be required. It will test how well your thyroid is working. Many that have mood swings actually have an under active thyroid. The good news is that if this is the problem, there are medications that can treat thyroid problems.

Still there is more to talk about with your doctor. You'll want to tell him about the medications that you are taking, as these can also cause a number of mood swings. For example, medications like corticosteroids including prednisone can cause mood swings. If you are being treated for depression with medications, or for anxiety, then your medication can lead to mood swings. The medications that are used to treat Parkinson's disease are also mood swing prone medications.

Your doctor will ask you about your diet, too. The foods you eat lead to the number of nutrients that you get. Those that are lacking in B 12 vitamins in particular can experience vast mood swings.

Any of these types of conditions can lead your doctor to determine that you are suffering from bipolar disorder. By talking with you and looking at the test results that are given to you, your doctor can determine exactly what is happening with you.

It is very important for you to communicate with your doctor about any of your needs and to be honest about your condition. By telling them about your daily life, including the bad parts, he or she can make the right decisions to help treat your conditions.

It is likely that you will find your doctor is quite experienced in bipolar disorder. That's because every year thousands of people see their doctors with worry about having this disorder. It is not as uncommon as you may think!

Once this has been done, your doctor and you can work on a treatment for your condition.

CHAPTER 2

BIPOLAR TREATMENT

Bipolar is a mental illness. Without the attention of a professional, your bipolar disorder can and will get worse.

What happens to you will be unique. There is no way of knowing if your condition will worsen quickly or at all. But, research shows that those that do not seek help for their condition will find complications do exist for them and for their family members.

If you have bipolar, other conditions can make it even worse. For example, if you are trying to deal with anxiety, you will have a hard time doing so because of bipolar. In conditions where this is life threatening, for example if you are suffering from alcoholism, this can be a very serious problem.

If you can't keep yourself off of alcohol, then your life may be in danger. Not only will the alcohol cause problems for your health, but bipolar can make you think irrationally and you could put yourself in dangerous situations. For this reason, seeking help is a must.

For some, the length of time between depressive symptoms and mania symptoms can be very short. You could move from one symptom to the next quickly, leading to confusion and even health scares. This rapid cycling in itself will cause you quite a bit of grief.

It can get even worse, too. It is possible, believe it or not, to be in a state of depression as well as in mania at the same time. When this happens, the end result is that your mind and emotions are completely wrapped in each other. You are agitated and annoyed. You are unable to sleep or eat. You can't get your thoughts to be organized.

Even worse, when this happens, people are more likely to think about suicide. This can be very dangerous because people in this state of mind are not thinking rationally at all and can make the wrong decision.

Another problem is that of psychosis. Bipolar symptoms that combine both mania and depression symptoms can lead to psychosis. This is a very serious mental illness in which your personality is completely disorganized. You are impaired with what is real and what is not. You are hallucinating and you are delusional. Even those that very strongly believe in things can end up making decisions the other way.

Stress & Anxiety

Even beyond the physical risks that you place yourself under when you face bipolar, there are the just as devastating effects that it has on your relationships.

Many people with bipolar will have trouble holding onto relationships. They may move from one person to the next quickly because of the mood swings that they deal with. In addition, those that are suffering from bipolar often times make mistakes with dealing with others. They simply are confused as to what the true emotion is supposed to be during any such situations.

In addition to this many with bipolar also have financial problems to boot. They do not make the right decisions regarding money, spending on credit and making choices in products. With this comes a number of problems from having to file bankruptcy to having to burden other family members with this problem.

Sometimes, a mania episode can trigger a shopping spree. Or a depressive episode can do the same just in the wrong way.

Still, one of the worst effects of bipolar is the way that people who have it treat themselves. Many find that the only way to cope with what is happening to them is to isolate themselves from everyone.

This happens easily during depressive phases especially when an individual is having a severe episode. Without the protection they need from a loved one, they can let their suicidal thoughts take control. Because of this isolation, it is important for those that have loved ones in this condition to provide them with the care that they need to keep them safe.

As you can see, the complications of bipolar disorder can be quite severe. Because many people that suffer from this condition simply do not realize that they have it, it can easily escalate and even put people in danger just doing the things that they do everyday.

The risk of driving a car, for example is very real. If a mania or depressive mood change happens, the person can easily loose control of the car. Even worse, they may make the wrong decisions in traffic, putting others at danger along with them. This scenario can be played out with many other situations in your life too.

Getting help, though, can really improve your outlook on life and reduce your risks and complications significantly.

CHAPTER 3

YOUR OPTIONS

As we've discussed, the first thing that you need to do is to talk with your doctor to determine what is affecting you. If it is in fact bipolar disorder, then there are several treatment options that your doctors will recommend to you.

The process of treating bipolar will come from two main forms, from your doctor that is. The first need is that of medication. The second is that of psychotherapy. The combination of these things has been effective in helping millions of people to improve their lives even while suffering from bipolar.

There is no cure for bipolar, but with the right treatments for the condition, you can increase your quality of life and keep yourself safe, too.

It is the combination of both medication and additional psychotherapy help that is the best route to go. Later, we will talk about other things that you can do beyond your doctor's care that can also aid in your improvement.

Medications

There are a number of different medications available that your doctor can prescribe to deliver some help to you. Medications have the goal of helping to regulate your mood swings.

The most common types of medications for mood control include Lithium in name brands such as Lithobid and Eskalith. These work as mood stabilizers and are actually one of the first tools to work against manic episodes. They are your first line of defense in regards to your mood swings.

In addition to these, there are other medications that are used to help stabilize the mood. Anti seizure medications in particular actually provide the help that's needed. These include medications like valproic acid with the brand name of Depakene. Divalproex, Iamotrigine also provide this same help.

They work as mood regulators. A less commonly used anti seizure medication is that of Topiramate which is sold as Topamax.

Yet, there is more help needed in the maintenance of the mood swings brought on by bipolar disorder. You probably will face episodes of depression and often times doctors find it important to handle these symptoms carefully.

They can actually be treated in a number of ways, though. Your doctor has several ways to go.

He may decide to give you antidepressants. Antidepressants are ideal for treating depression specifically and therefore often work with bipolar patients. These medications include a line of medications including:

- Paraxetine which is marketed as Paxil
- Buprpion which is marketed as Wellbutrin
- Fluoxetine which is marketed as both Proza and Sarafem
- Sertraline which is marketed as Zoloft

In addition to these, your doctor has the ability to provide you with antipsychotic medications if he deems that you need them. This includes two types including risperidone as Risperdal and olanzapine as Zyprexa.

Some medications have been created to treat both the depressive and the mania symptoms that you face with bipolar disorder. For example, just recently, the Food and Drug Administration approved quetiapine as Seroquel to treat both extents of your condition.

Yet, there are some concerns about medications that treat bipolar. There are some health risks that you can take on because you are taking these medications.

The American Diabetes Association has done research on several of these commonly used medications and has found that there are some very serious risks with them. For those that are taking antipsychotic medications, the risk that is highest is the development of diabetes.

In addition, you are prone to gaining weight to a very staggering level without the proper exercise and diet. In association with this, the increased weight can lead to increases in blood pressure which puts your heart at risk for problems.

This does not mean that you can't take these medications if your doctor tells you to. In fact, you must take them if your doctor tells you to because they can improve your life and health. But, you should always follow the recommendations of your doctor in regards to limitations as well as diet and exercise.

Some medications like Risperdal, Zyprexa and Seroquel are only used in severe bipolar conditions. Even then, your doctor will closely monitor your health in use of them. Doing this helps to keep the risks of complications at bay even when you take this medication regularly as you will for bipolar.

Each medication that you take will have different side effects and reactions. Some people find that medications offer no side effects to them while the same medication taken by someone else will have severe side effects.

When taking these medications for the first time, it is essential for you to take into consideration how they affect you. If you find that they are overwhelming or simply provide too severe of side effects, then contact your doctor right away so that he can tweak the dosage.

In addition, you should realize that medications often need some time in your system before you'll actually see any results. Some medications can take weeks of taking them daily before you notice their full benefit.

If it goes this long and you don't see any type of improvement, talk to your doctor. There should be another medication that will deliver the desired effects.

It will take some time before your doctor will be able to get the right dose for you. Be patient and work with your doctor as closely as you can to actually gain the benefits that you can have.

Psychotherapy

Although psychotherapy sounds like a pretty scary thing, it is actually something that can be done easily and with your help, it can be quite rewarding for you.

During psychotherapy, you and your doctor will work together to determine the best possible treatment for you. Usually, you'll be taking medications during this process. The combination can be quite beneficial to your overall health.

By meeting with a doctor to talk about psychotherapy, you both can learn more about your bipolar condition. The goal will be to find patterns in your episodes. By tracking and exploring the pattern of episodes that you go through, your doctor can better understand what triggers them.

By tracking your mood changes, the doctor can see if there is something that causes them in the first place. For example, if you take medications for some other condition, those medications may actually be triggering your mood changes and leading to the effect of bipolar.

Other common triggers include emotions. For example, if you have an argument with a loved one that is severe, then you may experience a mood swing that is severe. In addition to emotional causes, physical changes can also trigger your causes.

Just identifying these patterns is not enough, though. During psychotherapy, your doctor will work on finding ways for you to manage these episodes.

By learning to cope with the uncertainties that bipolar brings up, you can improve your overall well being.

Medication alone does not often bring the help that you'll need to deal with bipolar disorder. Those that face this condition need to learn how to realize that they are dealing with mood swings. Psychotherapy can help them to realize that they can cope with what's happening to them and stop hurting themselves and those around them.

It can also help you to realize the very importance of continuing to take your medications. When you realize the extent of what you do during your mood swings and how they are unfounded, you can learn to spot them and you'll realize that you need medication to help control them as much as possible.

Psychotherapy is something you should do on a continuing basis. By doing so, you allow yourself to get the most help that you can have.

Electroconvulsive Therapy

For those that have severe bipolar disorder, medications and psychotherapy may not be enough to provide them with the relief that they need.

Electroconvulsive therapy is another option that is available to you. You'll hear it called ECT more often.

Those that have electroconvulsive therapy generally have not responded well from the medications that have been used to help them. In addition, they generally have very severe depression in which suicidal thoughts are common. In cases where suicidal tendencies are seen, it can be important to seek additional treatment.

In electroconvulsive therapy, your doctor will use electrodes placed on your head to start the treatment. Your doctor will also give you a muscle relaxer during the treatment. When this is done, you'll be given anesthesia and you'll feel nothing.

Once this is done, the electrodes will admit a very small amount of electrical current. As the current passes through your brain, your brain will actually have a seizure. While in normal circumstances, a brain seizure can be very severe and very traumatic, that doesn't happen here.

Because you have taken a muscle relaxant, your body stays still and calm. The current only passes through your brain for less than a second.

But, why will this be done? There are actually not many answers to that question! During the process of electro convulsion, your brain will react in a very unique way. Your brain's metabolism changes significantly. The way that blood flows through your brain also changes. The end result is that the depression you face is lessened significantly and you feel better.

Although this has been proven to help ease depression and depression symptoms in cases such as bipolar disorder, it is not fully understood why this happens.

It can seem very troublesome to try this therapy. After all, it doesn't sound as if passing an electrical current through your brain is a beneficial thing.

But, remember that the amount of current and the time in which it passes into the brain are very, very small. That coupled with the control of the muscle relaxers, you end up benefiting from it instead of suffering from it.

What's Right For You?

Although we've presented several types of treatment for bipolar disorder, it will be up to you and your doctor to determine what the right course of action is for you. This decision will stem from your condition and its severity.

It also will take some time to adjust medications and to see benefits from psychotherapy. During that time, you may not be able to see much improvement. Yet, studies have shown benefits in the combination of medications and psychotherapy enough so that many patients see remarkable improvement in their daily lives.

By working with your doctor, you too can find this benefit. Yet, it will be important for you to do just that: work with your doctor. Stay in constant communication with him about how you are doing. He's there to help work out the wrinkles to find the best solution for you.

But, is that it? Is that all the help that you can get for your condition? No, and that's why this e-book is only half through. There are other ways that you can learn to cope with your condition.

CHAPTER 4

THE TRUTH ABOUT BIPOLAR DISORDER

Although medication and psychotherapy are methods for dealing with bipolar disorder, many times individuals simply will not take them. They stop. They give up. They simply cannot stand the entire process of fighting their bodies and minds. They just give up.

As you can probably imagine, this is simply not the best route for you to take when it comes to caring for your condition. Yet, a vast number of bipolar disorder patients will experience this feeling at some time or another. Why is that?

Those that take antipsychotic medications and mood stabilizers are often the types of medications with the most side effects and therefore the most commonly stopped by the patient.

Yet, those that just stop taking these medications against their doctor's recommendations often face a huge problem. They relapse in their symptoms. They are often hospitalized. They end up homeless, victims, and even are more commonly involved in various types of crime. Either in jail or in a hospital, those that do not have the medications they need end up in trouble.

Noncompliance And Nonadherence

When a patient stops taking their medication, this is called noncompliance or sometimes it is called nonadherence. It is not just those that suffer from bipolar disorder and take these medications that face this problem.

In fact, those that are told they need to take medications for long periods of time often go through a bout of not wanting to do so any longer. Those that suffer from epilepsy, hypertension and even asthma often face this feeling of wanting to stop the medications.

One thing to understand is that you don't have to stop taking all of your medications to face a problem. Some individuals only stop taking some of them; perhaps those that they still have pills available for, and stop others. Partial noncompliance is just as problematic as those that face cutting off all medications all together.

Nevertheless, this doesn't answer our question of why this happens. Unfortunately, there are a number of different reasons why it will happen.

You Don't Understand Your Illness

The first and most common reason that this happens is simply because patients don't understand the illness that they are up against. In fact, some 10 out of 14 patients will stop taking medications because they don't realize just how important they are to their illness.

Many patients, up to 80 percent, will take medications only because their doctor's tell them to. Many don't realize why they need to take the medications that they do, but simply do so because their doctor tells them to. Because people do this, it is hard to understand just how aware they are of their illness.

One of the most important things that you can do, then, is to truly understand your condition. If your loved one has bipolar disorder, then help them to stay informed about their condition. It is essential that you provide this information because without it, they may not realize the importance of taking those pills each day.

With this education, though, protection can be significant from these problems.

Dependency

Although lack of awareness about their condition is the single most common reason that patients do not take their medication, the dependency that they have on alcohol and drugs is another reason that it happens.

Those that put themselves in this position often are at a great risk of health related problems due to those medications. Many times, it becomes very important for a patient to make a choice. Should they take their medications or should they continue to drink alcohol or do drugs?

This decision is often one that happens because psychiatrists often tell their patients that they can't take their medications and drink at the same time.

This in itself is a very detrimental mixture. Mixing alcohol or illegal drugs with your medications can have severe health concerns.

Instead of deciding not to drink or do drugs, the addiction that many bipolar patients have to these substances keeps them consuming those instead of medications. This can be very detrimental to their well being, though.

For this reason, it is essential that patients pair medicinal treatment with substance abuse treatment at the same time in order to stop themselves from these types of situations which can ultimately lead to a health crisis.

They Don't Like The Doctor

Another reason why some bipolar patients stop taking their medications is as simple as they just don't like their psychiatrist. While this can be listed as a reason for not going to the doctor as you should, you should never stop taking your medications for this reason.

If you do not like your doctor or psychiatrist for any reason, seek out the help of another one. The move is simple and the end result is that you have the care that you need without risking your medication usage.

The Side Effects

Although many people believe that the side effects of medications is the reason why so many people stop taking their bipolar medications, studies have shown that this is not nearly as important as lack of understanding of their illness. Nevertheless, 10 percent of patients will stop taking medications because of the side effects associated with them.

The problem here is not that the medication is too harsh for you. The problem is not that the medication is the wrong one for you, either. The problem is that your dosage may be wrong. Too high or too low of a dose can lead to a number of extreme side effects. Working with your doctor, you can get this dosage right so that you improve your overall benefits.

It is common to hear that medications that are taken first, called first generation antipsychotic are often more prone to side effects than those that are taken when the first generation do not work. Medications like Seroquel and Abilify, Geordon and Zyprexa often have many fewer side effects than other medications.

In this regard, then, some doctors will change the medication that you are taking if they determine that the side effects you are facing are that severe.

If you talk with your doctor, you can easily find the right medication for your needs as well as for your side effect intensity. By working through the first few months with your doctor, the right medication will be found for your specific case.

What Else Can It Be?

There are many other reasons that people stop taking their medications. Those that don't see a very quick improvement in their symptoms don't take them long enough to realize their benefits. Some medications take weeks to actually see a result in their use.

Those that suffer from depression even in just bouts also often face the problem of not wanting to take their medications due to this factor. Those that face depression of any severity should have someone to help them to remember to take their medications for their own well being.

Some people don't take their medications because they don't have them. There is no doubt that medications are not cheap and when you can't afford them, you don't get them. This problem is one that needs to be addressed by your doctor, you and the financial aid that may be available to you through governmental offices.

Finally, some patients don't take their medication for bipolar disorder simply because they enjoy being in their manic stage. Still, this stage is only a stage and you are still putting yourself at risk of health related illness by not taking your medication!

CHAPTER 5

LEARNING TO COPE WITH BIPOLAR DISORDER

One of the biggest messages you need to take from this e-book is the fact that you can improve your condition if you make some changes in your lifestyle. You can learn to cope with bipolar disorder.

You may sit there and think to yourself that you just don't want to deal with this. You may want to be able to write it off as an "Oh well." But, in fact, you've seen reasons why you can do that. Now, that you realize that, take the time to realize what changes you can make in your life to actually improve your overall quality of life.

Don't try to make all of these changes today. Give yourself time and patience to work through each one. Doing so will give you more ability to actually be successful with coping with bipolar disorder.

In this chapter, we talk about a number of simple ways that you can improve your quality of life by learning coping techniques. Take them one step at a time but try to get them all worked into your lifestyle. They seem simple because they can be just that.

The Way You Sleep

Believe it or not, the way that you sleep plays a significant role in your bipolar condition. What's important to remember here is that when you sleep in a normal pattern, there are chemical changes in the brain that are beneficial to your condition.

To improve this condition, simply get enough sleep each night, but do this by going to bed about the same time each night and get up about the same time each morning. Creating a pattern like this will improve your bipolar symptoms.

If you work a job that has you sleeping strange times of the day, you need to try to work out a schedule so that even when you are not working, you are still sleeping the same times of the day. This is essential to your coping skills. It also gives your mind the time that it needs to clear and to wake up refreshed.

In fact, when you do need to make changes in your sleep pattern that are drastic, such as a new time zone, talk to your doctor about the best way to do this without causing problems for yourself.

Monitor Your Medications

We've talked a lot about taking the medications that you need to take and the reasons for doing so. But, you can also learn to cope with this process to make it that much more successful for you.

Take your medications even if you feel great. Do what your doctor tells you to do in regards to taking them even when you have no symptoms. Even if you feel really good, that's your medication talking and working! By stopping the consumption of them, you simply allow the symptoms to begin all over again.

To make the entire process of medication taking easy plan out your schedule so as to include your dosing. For example, when you wake up in the morning, have your breakfast and take your morning pills. If you take a second pill later in the day, do so after dinner, for example. By pairing medication taking with meals, for example, you keep yourself from forgetting them.

If you do take more than one pill and are easily confused by them (and who wouldn't be?) purchase a pill organizer and use this to portion out your medications. Those that are for a week or even a month at a time are excellent tools to insure that you don't forget and don't become confused with medications.

Another tip to remember about your medications is that they don't mix well. If you get a cold, consult your doctor about which cold medications you can take with your bipolar medications. You should never mix them with any type of alcohol or other drugs.

If another doctor prescribed medications for you, don't take them until you are fully sure that they are aware of the bipolar medications that you are taking. If and when medications are mixed, they can interact with each other and even bring on extreme conditions including health crisis like events.

Maintain Your Level Of Activity

An important part of managing bipolar disorder is to completely organize and regulate your life in the best way that you can. For those that are used to working very hard, every day, this may mean pulling back some to a normal paced activity level.

No matter what you do, by regulating the amount that you do the same or about the same each day, you also help to ease those chemicals in your brain and therefore avoid the symptoms that can sometimes happen when you are frantically running around one day and doing nothing but watching television the next day!

Don't Use Drugs Or Alcohol

The temptation to use alcohol and drugs is very strong for many people. When you are dealing with the symptoms of bipolar disorder, you may feel the need to just relax. Turning to alcohol or drugs can be a huge temptation. The mood swings may feel better while you are intoxicated, but the mixture of medications with these substances can be fatal. Some will take alcohol and drugs to help them to sleep. The problem is that it almost always makes it even worse.

If you have problems with alcohol and drugs, seeking help and counseling will help to provide you the strength that you need to overcome this problem. One of the best tools to use is that of Alcoholics Anonymous or other self help groups. We'll talk more about their benefits in just a minute.

The use of alcohol, caffeine and even over the counter medications can be deadly and can cause enough medical trouble for you to land you in the hospital. This is especially true for over the counter cold medications and allergy medications. Always check with your doctor about the right medications to use when you are ill.

In addition to that, realize that these over the counter medications and trigger mood swings, even when you are taking your medication.

They can interfere with your sleep patterns, cause loss of appetite and put your body in the position of being vulnerable. If you become sick, talk to your doctor about the best medications for your condition.

Caffeine offers the same type of trigger and keeps you from getting sleep, too. If you feel that you need coffee in the morning, you need to find a decaffeinated coffee or stop drinking it all together. Just a small amount of this type of product daily is all that it will take to limit the effectiveness of your medications.

- Don't use alcohol
- Don't use illegal drugs

- Cut as much caffeine related products like soda, coffee and chocolate out of your diet.

- Ask your doctor which over the counter medications are okay for you to use with your current prescription medications and those that will not cause problems with mood swings and sleep depravation.

Doing those four things can drastically improve the quality of life that you have. Although it may seem hard to not be able to have a drink, you know that the benefits of not having to deal with mood swings matters more.

Support

Getting support from your family is vitally important. Many bipolar patients like to think that they can do it on their own. But, as we've discussed, it is very difficult to do this. Most of the time, you won't realize how severe your mood swing is. You may not realize that you are lashing out at a loved one for no reason.

Step one is to tell those that you love about your bipolar disorder. As difficult as that sounds, those close to you can be your safety net. They can help you to realize what is happening and how you are acting. A supportive person will guide you to help and will stand by you through this prognosis and this life long challenge.

Step two is to realize that you aren't the only one that is suffering. Bipolar patients often lash out at those that they love. Those in your family have to deal with mood swings that can be quite severe. Although you feel you can't do much about this, helping your loved ones to be educated and informed about your condition will reduce the amount of stress that plays along with bipolar disorder.

If they know what you are suffering from, they can help you. If they don't, they don't understand why you are doing what you are doing. That leads to family stress and painful situations. Without an understanding of what is happening, your family just can't be as supportive as they could be otherwise.

In addition to just having knowledge of the effect that bipolar disorder has on you, you should also seek out the help that you need from a family therapist. Even a family that doesn't have much strife in it will need to get the help and support of a therapist. Bipolar disorder causes trauma in families and having this additional help is a saving grace in the way of understanding.

Finally, when an educated family can support the person that is suffering from bipolar disorder, he or she can strive for improvement with help. The family can provide support when mood swings take over.

And, they can help to keep you and your doctor informed about the way that you react to situations, to mood swings and even to your medications. That adds up to a successful situation for the bipolar disorder patient.

The family unit is a tool that all bipolar disorder patients need, but many times you may feel the desire to simply run and hide. You may feel as if you would rather be alone. Getting through that feeling will lead to success.

Reduction Of Stress

Just reading the title of this section you are thinking to yourself that you can't do it. You've heard it before. You know that stress is a killer of many people, not just those that suffer from bipolar disorder. Yet, it is essential that you look at your life and identify those times when stress has lead to mood swings or even out of control behaviors that put you at risk.

Consider this. If you push yourself at work to be the person that does the most, what do you accomplish? You probably will cause the onset of numerous symptoms of bipolar disorder specifically that of mood swings. When this happens, you put yourself in a position of not being able to work or even worse putting your position at jeopardy.

Therefore, you end up not actually benefiting from all of your hard work, but instead have fewer benefits and ultimately you drop the productivity level that you could have had.

On the other hand, if you would have worked a steady schedule and done what you should have done in regards to stress management, you ultimately would have accomplished more.

Here are some tips for stress management at work.

- Work the same hours as much as possible. By working a predicable and steady schedule allows you to stick to a schedule which helps to lessen mood swings.

- Get the rest that you need. You need to try to sleep at the same time each day. You need to be able to monitor your sleep patterns to reduce mood swings.

- When you are suffering from mood swings, consider whether or not you should be working. For some, it may mean talking with your doctor about how they affect your job. Ultimately, you need to decide if you are benefiting yourself or not by continuing to work and tough out these mood swings.

- Take time off. Those that take time off often improve their overall health and well being. By getting time off each week and even vacation time, (or taking time off when you need to) you improve your level of stress and how the body reacts to it.

- Don't work in overly stressful environments. While you may not feel that this is something that you can control, it needs to be. Those that suffer with bipolar need to consider their health above anything else. Mood swings, depressive and manic symptoms, can be made worse when you put yourself in a position to deal with a lot of stress.

- Work through problems. If there are small things that happen that cause you to worry or cause stress, handle them right away. Small problems turn into large ones that are much less likely to be dealt with. By handling problems quickly, you reduce the stress toll that they take on you ultimately.

Reducing stress should be one of the most important things that you do. By doing so, you lessen the risk of having a mood swing because of stress.

Learn to spot stressful situations and learn how to get out of them effectively! It will pay off.

Watch For Signs

Believe it or not, learning to watch for signs of the onset of mood swings can be an excellent tool to aid you in coping with your illness. The early warning signs of an episode can be seen before they become full blown swings.

Why do you want to actually pay attention to this? There are a number of benefits that can come from you seeing and taking action when you see them.

Unfortunately, your doctor can only give you an idea of what will happen to you during a mood swing. That's because each person is unique and that in itself provides for challenges. Each person will move from depressive symptoms to manic symptoms differently and at different times.

The faster you notice that your mood is changing, the faster you can take action to prevent it or at least to deal with what is coming. The faster you do this, the faster help can get to you.

What are the warning signs? Here are some things that can be a small mood change that ultimately can be a predictor of a large mood swing behind the next door. Learn to notice these to spot mood changes.

- **Sleep changes.** If you are on a sleep pattern (which you should be) when you notice that you can't sleep or you are tired even after getting a full nights rest, this can be a predictor of a mood swing.

- **Energy level.** Fluctuations in energy levels are a strong indicator that you are having a mood change. Since most of the time mania will incorporate increased energy while depressive symptoms take away, you can see how this could be spotted.

- **Loss of sexual interest.** Some patients will encounter times when they don't want any type of sexual touching. Although it is common for people to be interested and not interested normally, a change that is significant should be noted.

- **Concentration.** You go to work and get the job done. Sometimes, you may have a feeling that you just can't stay on task. When you feel that you can't concentrate and finish the tasks that you started, this can be a sign of a mood change.

- **Self esteem.** It is important for family members to take notice of these situations. If you or your loved one determines that you are down and out or you are saying negative things about yourself, then this could be a sign that depressive symptoms are coming. It is essential that these things be spotted and treated as soon as possible.

- Thought changes. If you just for no reason seem to be very optimistic, or you are thinking about death a lot, this can be a sign that you are having a mood swing. If these thoughts turn suicidal, it is imperative to seek help as soon as possible.

- **Changes in the way you appear.** Some bipolar disorder patients will go through stages in which they feel as if they need to change the way that they look. You may change the way that you groom or to the level that you groom. You may all of a sudden hate the clothes that you have. These can be signs of a mood swing because of the emotion that is often attached to them.

The early warning signs of a mood swing can be wonderful tools to aid you in spotting trouble before it happens, or at least to the degree that it can happen. But, one of the problems with this is that most people can't spot these things on their own. They often see these stresses as just their everyday lifestyle.

For this reason, it is important that family members be able to spot these early warning signs and then help you to get through them. By spotting changes in you, your family can help you to get some help and quickly!

What should be done if you experience some of these mood changes? If you notice the warning signs, you should contact your doctor as soon as possible to find the relief that you need. He or she can offer supportive help that extends to medication if he deems it necessary.

This also can be helpful in spotting patterns of mood swings and that can be a tool to long term treatment as well.

Keep Your Doctor Informed

Although you may hate to go to the doctor and you may think that your doctor never has anything good to say, it is very important to keep him informed. By telling him what is going on and what you are feeling, he can make better decisions for you.

You should contact your doctor:

- When you feel that a mood swing is going to happen sometime soon.

- When you feel that you are experiencing a mood swing

- When your medications are not working the way that you thought they were supposed to

- When you have any type of suicidal thoughts, feelings of despair or are having trouble getting through the day without feeling sad.

- When your family members tell you that you are going through a mood swing or they tell you that you are showing signs of either mania or depressive symptoms due to their understanding.

Your doctor can help you to learn to cope with these situations. They can also prescribe medication differences that can also act as a tool to improving your health and well being.

By keeping your doctor informed, you allow your symptoms to be monitored. Your doctor can learn patterns and even notice the things that trigger these episodes to happen. That can lead to benefits throughout your lifetime including the avoidance of those situations which will lead to fewer episodes throughout your lifetime.

Learning to cope with bipolar disorder is a must. By taking a look at your life right now, you'll be able to see things that can be changed that will ultimately improve your well being. Do you sleep right? Do you eat right? Do you know what your early warning signs are? Taking care of these changes now will ultimately improve your overall well being.

You can learn to cope with bipolar disorder. Now, there are a few more things you can do too.

CHAPTER 6

SUPPORT GROUPS

Everyone hates them and not one wants to go to support groups. But, think about why that is. Is it too hard for you to do? Do you hate admitting that something could be wrong? Perhaps you are like one of the many that actually find themselves struggling with the need to surround yourself with others that face the same challenges that you do.

The bottom line is that support groups do help and that they commonly can help to increase your quality of life and help you to realize what you are up against.

Learning to cope with bipolar disorder is not easy but it is challenging. It is something that you can learn to do. In fact, one of the best ways to do this is to work with others that are facing the same situations that you are.

Support groups offer that type of care, something that your family and friends can not give you nor can your doctor. Being around others that are struggling with the same problems you are struggling with, gives you hope, understanding and even a sense of peace.

Who Is Your Support Group?

Learning about support groups is vitally important. Who is in yours depends on your family make up and even those that are striving to provide you with the care that you need.

Right now, you probably have a family that is helping to support your needs. You also have a health care team that is there to provide you with medical assistance. This includes everyone from your family doctor to the psychiatrist that you've poured your heart out to.

Friends should make up part of your support group too. Many don't want to provide personal information about themselves such as their bipolar disorder, but the fact is that you should. A true friend stays by you and helps you to cope as well as offers you the support you need in all times of your life.

Consider telling those that you love what is happening to you. It can only benefit you. What's more, it can help people to understand the way that you react and the moods that you go through, making you a better friend to them.

Outside Support

While having your family around you will improve your well being and will offer the help that you need, you should consider additional help through outside support groups as well.

Professional groups that meet to discuss bipolar disorder are found in many hospitals, recreation centers and in various psychiatric facilities. To find one that is located near you, ask your doctor for suggestions. They may have one that is tailored to your specific needs in mind for you to choose to got to based on your situation.

These support groups provide professional attention that can be guided by you. For example, several people that have the same disorder as you do can come together with a moderator. By sharing the ins and outs of your day with others, you help them to improve their life as much as you'll help yourself to do the same.

Bipolar disorder is a condition where isolation leads to worsening symptoms. A therapy group will provide you with the needs that you have in meeting others that have your same symptoms. It helps you to know that others out there are going through the same things that you are. It is excellent help in realizing that you aren't alone in what you are facing.

If that is still not enough to get you to a support group, the fact that many of those that do attend them actually find a reduction in their symptoms should! By being able to talk about your stresses and your problems, you increase the amount of time between your episodes of mood swings.

Not only will you be getting benefits from outside support group members, but you also provide them to others. No one else can understand the frustration of not being able notice your mood swings.

No one else can feel the frustration of feeling down and depressed and not knowing why. And, no one else can understand fully the problems with taking medications and the sheer fact that you'll live with bipolar disorder for the rest of your life.

By utilizing support from both your family and friends and outside support groups, you can gain a level of understanding and benefit. Bipolar disorder may be holding you against your will, but with support from outside sources, you can fight against the effect that it has on your daily and long term life.

CHAPTER 7

COPING BY MONITORING SYMPTOMS:
THE MOOD CHART

Coping with bipolar disorder is something that you should do in many ways. One of those ways, as we have discussed includes monitoring your symptoms. While we discussed several reasons why you need to watch for the early signs and symptoms of bipolar, it is also important for you to see how your treatment is working.

To monitor your own treatment of bipolar disorder, you need to use a mood chart. There are several useful, easy and quite effective ways that you can do this. A mood chart helps you to track the way that you feel on any given day. By keeping track of this, you can better see the ups and downs of your condition.

Your doctor may ask you to keep a mood chart especially at the beginning of your treatment. But, it is best to continue with it for the long term because it provides you, your family, your friends and your doctors with help in spotting episodes of mood changes. When all of these individuals can pull together, you'll see remarkable benefits in your daily life.

What Is It?

A mood chart is a simple diary. You will use it to keep track of your mood changes, your daily feelings, the things that you do and the way that you sleep. It is quite an effective tool when put to good use. Here's what to include in your mood chart for starters:

1. The way that you feel that day, including any feeling changes. If you wake up in a great mood, record this. If later someone angers you, record this too.

2. Your activities also need to be recorded. If you go to work, write it down. If you decide to spend the day in bed, this too needs to be recorded. Being able to track the things that you do will help you and your doctor to spot triggers and to spot oncoming severe mood swings.

3. Sleep patterns are very important to the bipolar patient. You should track the changes that happen in your sleeping because it will trigger differences in your overall well being.

4. Medications and side effects should also be considered daily. If you take your medication and in an hour feel like you need a nap, this should be recorded. It is very important to remember to include changes in your overall response, too. If you begin to have new side effects or ones that are worsened, this needs to be considered.

5. Life changes and life events that are significant should be noted. Sometimes, the death of a loved one or the stresses at work can lead to mood changes that can be severe.

Most days, you'll record a normal day. Many times you won't have a lot of details to incorporate into your mood chart. Other times, though, you may find the need to include many details.

There are a number of different types of charts on the market that can be quite useful to you. Select one that your doctor tells you is the right choice. It will ultimately provide you with the best record of how to manage your mood swings by keeping track of them.

If you don't want to do this on paper, you can make a virtual diary on a document that you keep on your computer too. To remember to do this tracking, simply take note of it the same time each day, perhaps after you eat a meal. Diarize it! You'll be rewarded with the answers that you need for daily life management.

CONCLUSION

FINAL WORDS

Bipolar disorder is a life long illness that affects millions of people each year. Most of them go on to live normal and happy lives because they learn the coping skills they need to empower themselves.

You have a choice. You can choose to live a happy and full life that makes you happy by making sacrifices now or you can continue to make decisions that affect the quality of your life and those that you love. While the road to a good life can be one that is filled with struggles and often the feeling of having to give things up, it is one that will ultimately reward you with a longer, healthier life.

These coping methods are just the start of your journey. Soon you'll be able to see the things that effect you yourself and you'll be able to rein them in.

You can improve the quality of your life by simply managing these aspects of it.

You are worth the work it takes to improve. You alone can make the decision to change.

———————————

Printed by Libri Plureos GmbH in Hamburg, Germany